For my three little bears.
May your dreams always be sweet and your lives
full of adventure.

For Ali.
Thank you for your love, motivation, and support.

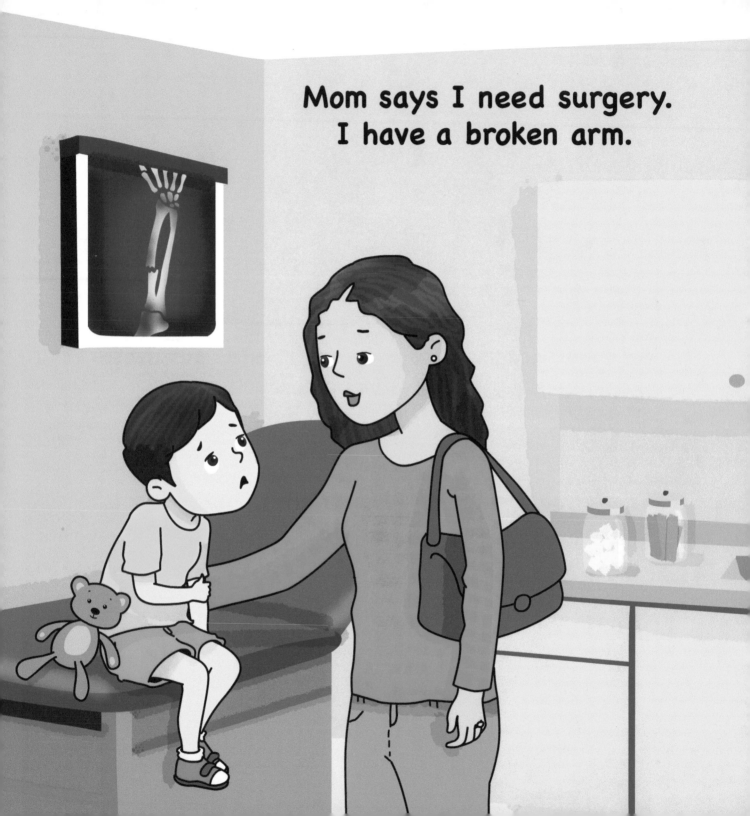

Mom says I need surgery.
I have a broken arm.

I swung too high,
jumped too far,

and caused myself
some harm.

The waiting room has others
who are sick or had a fall.

My parents talk to people that wear silly hats and masks.

I'm not sure what's going on, but I hope we get home fast.

They tell me they will fix my arm while I take a nice nap.

It's time to change into a gown and my puffy blue cap.

The doctor looks at me and says,
"Don't worry about a thing. Is that a
stuffed bear that you would like to bring?"

I squeeze my bear tightly
and drink a sleepy juice.

Before I know it, I'm down the hall
and giggling like a goose!

Here we are, the operating room. They say I have one task...

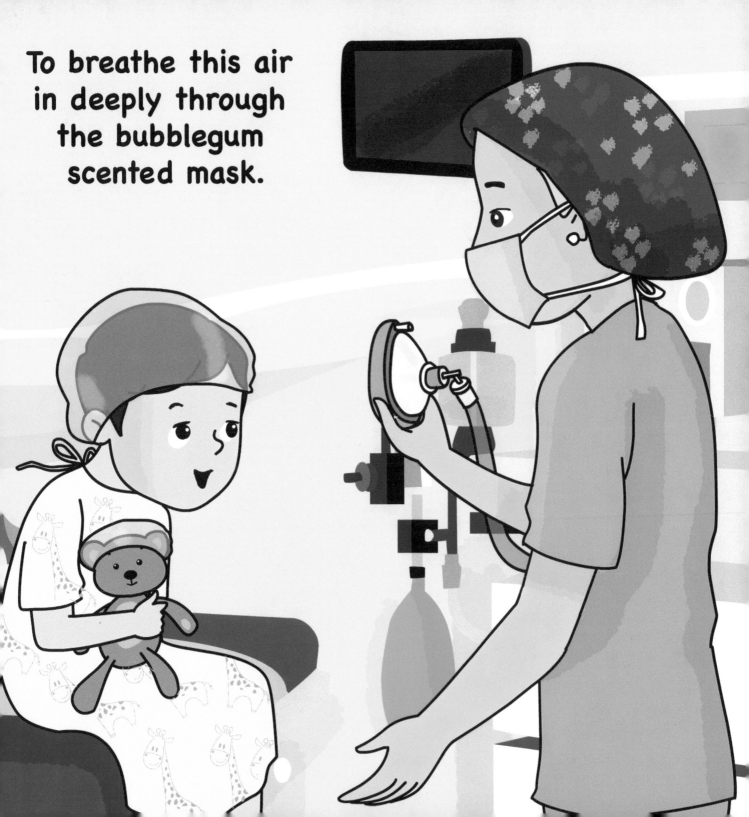

To breathe this air in deeply through the bubblegum scented mask.

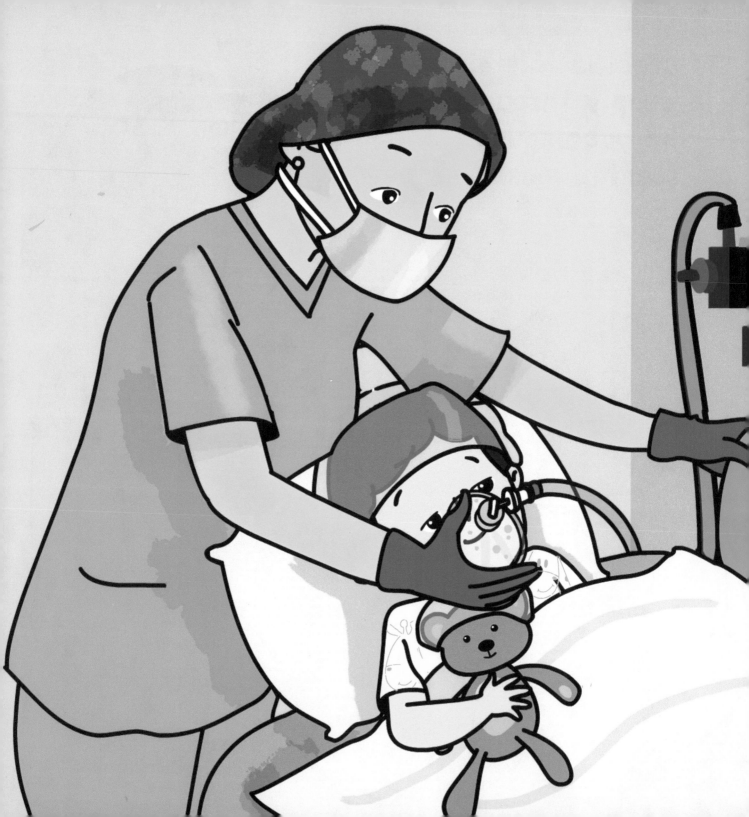

As I start to fall asleep,
I begin to wonder,
what I could pretend to be
as I'm going under?

I dream that I'm an astronaut
launching into space.
In my giant spaceship,
I can travel any place.

Maybe I'll go to the Moon
or even visit Mars.
Or maybe I'll just fly around
and say hi to all the stars.

Next, I am a diver on an underwater mission.
I think the fish are talking, but I find
it hard to listen.

Their bright colors surround me like
a rainbow in the sea. While swimming
with the fish, I'm as happy as can be.

Before I know it, I'm waking up with
my arm in a cast.
Mom and Dad have signed it and I say,
"I had a blast!"

Now that I'm awake,
the nurse says I'll get a treat.
I can choose a popsicle
or something sweet to eat.

"Let's go home," I say.
"I have so much to tell my friends."
Like how the doctor helped me sleep
and how I'll start to mend.

I'll tell about the hospital and the people in funny clothes. Most of all, I'll tell of my adventures while I dozed.

The End

For all correspondence:
Sleepy Tale Publishing
sleepytalepublishing@gmail.com

Second Printing, 2019

Library of Congress Control Number: 2019903291
ISBN 978-0-578-47933-0

CPSIA information can be obtained
at www.ICGtesting.com
Printed in the USA
BVHW020829240122
627016BV00007B/296